WORK SUCKS!

A Hilarious Guide to Choosing
or Changing Your Career

by

Bob Glickman

Illustrated by Walter Strump

CCC PUBLICATIONS • LOS ANGELES

Published by

CCC Publications
21630 Lassen St.
Chatsworth, CA 91311

Copyright © 1992 Bob Glickman

All rights reserved by CCC Publications. No part of this book may be reproduced or transmitted in any form or by any means, electronic or mechanical, including photocopying, recording or by any information storage and retrieval system, without the written permission of the publisher, except where permitted by law. For information address: CCC Publications; 21630 Lassen St., Chatsworth, CA 91311.

Manufactured in the United States Of America

Cover © 1992 CCC Publications

Cover art by Don Vernon

Illustrations © 1992 Walter Strump & CCC Publications

Interior art by Walter Strump

Interior layout & production by Tim Bean/
DMC Publishing Group

ISBN: 0-918259-42-8

If your local U.S. bookstore is out of stock, copies of this book may be obtained by mailing check or money order for $5.95 per book (plus $2.50 to cover postage and handling) to:
CCC Publications; 21630 Lassen St. Chatsworth, CA 91311.

Pre-publication Edition - 8/92

DEDICATION

To my siblings: David—the professional comedian, Betsy—the CPA, and Penny—the doctor. I can't imagine how I ever came up with the idea for this book.

Thank you for your inspiration and the years of unwavering belief in "Bobby."

PREFACE

A new career.

Experts agree that finding a new career can be one of the most emotionally-jarring endeavors we humans ever face.

Experts, Shmexperts. What do **they** know?

An Expert is just a person who was too straight-laced to become a Rock Star, too efficient to become a Postal Worker, and too ethical to become a Lawyer. Under different circumstances, that "Expert" might have been "Inspector #2" at a major underwear firm.

The point is, there are **oodles** of ways to make a living. If you don't like what you're doing, you can choose something else!

It's like my mom and dad used to say to me, "Bob, you can be anything you want—just don't tell anyone we're your parents."

This guide is designed to help you choose a new, more satisfying way of spending your waking hours. On the other hand, it also may help you realize that your current job isn't too bad, and that your bi-hourly thoughts of "WORK SUCKS!" may not be completely justified.

After carefully studying the contents of the book, you should be in good shape to find a career you like.... A career that helps you answer with pride and confidence when some goober asks you that inevitable question, "So, uh, whadaya do?"

B.G.

HOW TO USE THIS BOOK

1) Open the book. (Just Testing!)
   Proceed immediately to Step 2.)

2) Find a job title that sounds interesting. (They're in alphabetical order.) Read the description that follows the job title and ask yourself:
   A) Is this job for me?

   B) Could I do this job?

   C) What would my friends think?

   D) Do I **have** any friends?

3) Repeat Step 2 for other jobs titles. Then Rinse.

CTOR

-A person who tells people he's an Actor, usually just after telling them he'll be back in a moment for their order.

ADVERTISING EXECUTIVE
-If you're tired of TV shows interrupting your favorite commercials, you're just weird enough to fit in here.

ADVERTISING EXECUTIVE, SUBLIMINAL
-If you're tired of TV shows interrupting your favorite commercials, you're just weird BUY THIS BOOK enough to fit in here.

AERIAL PHOTOGRAPHER
-You will constantly be asked to photograph outdoor weddings made up of extraordinarily obese people.

AEROBICS INSTRUCTOR
-Recent medical studies show that prolonged jumping up and down jars the brain just enough to cause utter stupidity. Of course, if you're **already** somewhat of an airhead, there's no risk involved.

AGENT, ENTERTAINMENT
-The only member of the lizard family to wear a coat and tie.

AIR TRAFFIC CONTROLLER
-This is the next step for bored video game enthusiasts. Look at all the bleeps and blurbs on the screen, and see if you can keep them apart!

AIRLINE BAGGAGE HANDLER
-This position is actually supervised by a powerful union— **Worldwide Handlers Of Other Persons' Suitcases (WHOOPS)** — which requires members to lose and/or severely damage eight out of every ten pieces of luggage. One fringe benefit here is participating each year in the Baggage Handlers Olympics, where you can compete in events such as: **The Samsonite Toss, The Hide & Forget It**, and the **It Goes To Cleveland Unless My Tip Is At Least Ten Bucks.**

AIRLINE GROUND CREWMAN
-If you like power, this is the job for you. By simply waving your arms, you can direct a 747!.... Or, when nobody's watching, you can hold your arms out straight and pretend to **be** a 747.

AIRLINE PILOT
-If you can maneuver a 200,000-pound airplane while sounding over the cabin P.A. system like you're reclining in front of a fireplace listening to a Sinatra record, this profession was made for you. Most importantly, if you're ever laid off, you can use that mellow voice to do the late-night shift on FM jazz stations.

ANCHORPERSON, NEWS
-This career requires that rare skill known as **Happy Talk**, the lighthearted segues between news segments. If you can go from a grizzly mass murder to the Weather segment without a hitch, you're a master (i.e. "...At last count, fifty-nine people have died. And Walter, I thought I was going to die from that heat today.")

ANESTHESIOLOGIST
-Your job is to put people into a deep sleep with the injection of your drugs, and shock them back to reality with the arrival of your bill.

ANIMAL BREEDER
-This job sometimes entails showing the animals **how** to breed. To what extent that demonstration is carried out depends on the laws of the state (Georgia is most lenient) and the length of time since the Breeder's last date.

ANIMAL HOSPITAL OWNER
-A highly profitable business. By recognizing the true love many people have for their pets, you can rake them over the coals with ridiculous treatments they'll feel too guilty to turn down.

ANIMAL TRAINER
1) You will attempt to keep a dozen 400-pound lions and tigers from eating you by holding a stool in one hand and a rope in the other. Have fun.
2) School Teacher, New York City.

ANNOUNCER
-That's right! You too can become an announcer. But wait— there's more!! You can also do voice-over work and public service announcements. But wait! Don't sign up yet! If you act now, you can learn to annoy people by talking like this all the time!!

ANTIQUE DEALER
1) Your job consists of going to the dump, finding a piece of junk, bringing it back to your shop, and putting a price tag of $345 on it.
2) A very old drug trafficker.

APARTMENT MANAGER
-A Magician of sorts, in that you make a tenant's security deposit vanish into thin air for no apparent reason.

ARCHAEOLOGIST
-(aka Bone Digger.) This is the only career that if you're out sick, your dog can go in and cover for you.

ARCHITECT
-In this field, you're required to have **very** long arms. You need them to carry around that huge rectangular blueprint case which averages 5 feet by 12 feet.

ARMY DRILL INSTRUCTOR
-Here's a person who isn't familiar with the word **Decaffeinated**.

ART DIRECTOR
-An excellent alternative to growing up. These people make a living by doing what we all did in kindergarten—drawing.

ARTIST
-An often brilliant individual who balances his time between creative thought, skillful implementation, and standing in the unemployment line.

ASTROLOGER
-What might be looked upon as circumstances involving this vocation or occupation could ultimately change, enabling loved ones to learn of impending stability. Those close to you will play a major role in a CBS mini-series. Financial situation remains generic.

ASTRONAUT
-The adult Space Cadet. If things on Earth are a little too mundane for your tastes, get your butt to a launch pad and become a high-tech hermit.

ASTRONOMER
-If things on Earth are a little too mundane for your tastes, but you're a little too fat to fit in a space shuttle, become an Astronomer. This way, you can at least **look** into space.

ATTORNEY
-A Lawyer with an attitude. *(See Lawyer)*

AUDIOLOGIST
1) This doctor tests your hearing by telling you how much he charges for an office visit, and then noting whether you say the words, "Are you kidding?"
2) A physician who drives an Audi.

AUDITOR
-You're the Auditor type if the analytical portion of your mind is always going strong, while your social skills are equivalent to that of a tortoise.

AUTO PLANT WORKER, AMERICAN
-A good vocation, in that your union assures you'll be paid at least $37 an hour to push a button marked ON.

BABYSITTER
-How else can you get paid to watch TV and raid a stranger's refrigerator?

BAIL BONDSMAN
-If honesty is important to you, your customers may disappoint you.

BAKER
-If you can eat and eat and never gain an ounce, you've found your calling. Otherwise, by the third week of work, your thighs will resemble Wyoming.

BANK EXAMINER
-When looking at bank records, you must have enough self-control not to reveal to all your friends that the town power broker actually has only $3.27 to his name.

BANK MANAGER
-Your job is to make sure the pen at the end of the little chain never works.

BANK SECURITY GUARD
-You must be at least sixty-five years old, at least forty pounds overweight, and talk about your grandchildren to anyone who will listen, so in case of an actual robbery, you could bore the criminals into surrendering.

BANK TELLER
-In this business, it's your job to casually hit the silent alarm button if you see someone enter the bank wearing a ski mask. Of course, you'll probably be considered a real pain in the ass if you work in Alaska.

BARBER
-If you refuse to accept the fact that times are-a-changing, you'll feel right at home in the corner barbershop. Same look and smell as in 1936, and Earl's still at that end chair.

BARTENDER
-Your job is to mix drinks just strong enough so the customers feel comfortable telling you their problems, but not so strong that they expect you to solve them.

BEGGAR, PANHANDLER
-If you don't have a job, but you're too good-natured to steal, this is the perfect solution. In fact, if you're real good at it, you can even become a Televangelist.

BELLHOP
-If you live for old Jerry Lewis movies, and you believe silliness should abound, you can have a ball being a Bellhop....***LADY!!***

BEST BOY
-In this role, you will work on a movie set doing something which is obviously kept secret from the outside world. But advancement is common, and soon, you could be promoted to Best Man.

BLACKSMITH
-In this trade, you bend steel the old-fashioned way, without the aid of large, modern machinery. On a good day, you may be able to turn out two, maybe three horseshoes. (A large inheritance is helpful in this career.)

BODYGUARD
-It's your job to throw your body between your client and any opposing force, such as a bullet. A key to one's effectiveness here is having a big body and little self-esteem.

BOOKKEEPER
-A great job for a partygoer. You can approach total strangers, tell them that your occupation is unique in having three sets of double letters in a row, and then challenge them to come up with others. ***Hours*** of Bookkeeper fun.

BOOKMOBILE DRIVER
-You must know the difference between your Hueys, Louies, and Deweys.

BOOKSTORE SALESPERSON
-Often a lover of literature, this individual is responsible for the arrangement of books, so offerings such as HUMOROUS CAREER CHOICE PARODIES can be placed on the shelf (in both the Business **and** Humor sections) with the front cover **facing** the prospective buyer.

BOSS
-As a general guideline, notice that **Boss** spelled backwards includes the letters S-O-B.

BOTANIST
-This is a natural field for you if you not only **talk** to plants, but you believe they've replied in confidence that they're planning a massive march on Washington next Arbor Day.

BOUNCER
-Can't memorize the football playbook? Does that grade of D in your high school "Intro to Addition" class detract from your resume? When walking, do you have to think, "Left. Right. Left. Right."? Perhaps you should look into this position.

BRAIN SURGEON
-A noble profession, but it just won't fly at singles bars. *Suuuuure* you're a Brain Surgeon.

BRICKLAYER
-Nothing is wrong with this occupation, but the title has gotta go. It brings to mind images that are entirely too sleazy for this wholesome book.

BUDGET DIRECTOR, U.S.
-This individual knows enough about the economy to be interviewed on the national news, but doesn't know enough about it to *improve* things.

BUM, LAZY
-If you've ever realized that *Elvis* is spelled out in the word TELEVISION, you've got just enough free time on your hands to officially be a Lazy Bum.

BURGLAR
-On the down side, working in this capacity generally means public disrespect, bad hours, and no health plan. But it all seems worth it when tax time rolls around.

BUS DRIVER

-The person in this role is often thought of as a Ralph Kramden type—overweight and pathetic. But the truth is, you need not be overweight.

BUSBOY

-Here's that lifelong career for those who found high school shop class a bit too challenging.

BUTCHER

-Tired of those annoying all-natural vegetarians permeating our society with health-conscious garbage? Get back to what real humans are all about—red meat and heart disease. Be a Butcher, damn it!

BUTLER

-You'd better have a good Lawyer on retainer, because history tells us that if any criminal mischief occurs, you did it.

BUYER

-Does your body start to quiver with excitement at the word Sale? Can you instantly determine 30% off *infinity*? Do you consider Neiman Marcus and Macy's to be erogenous zones? Why not get paid for all the fun?—This *is* your calling.

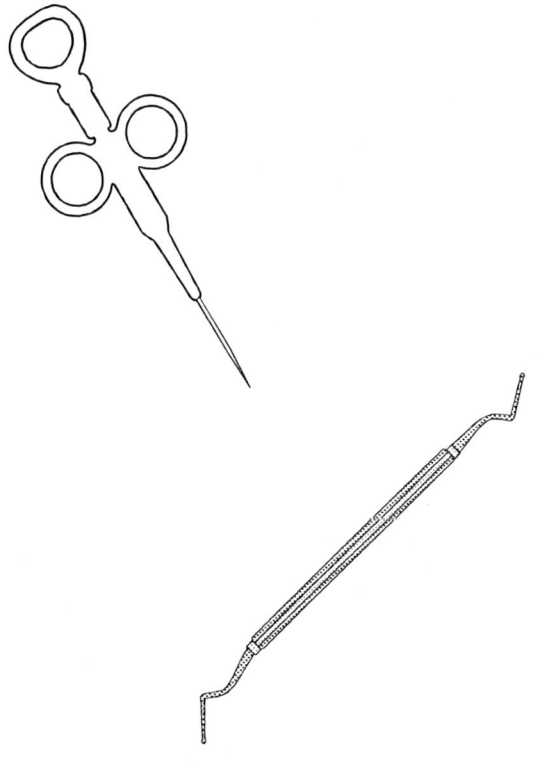

CAB DRIVER
-An immigrant who moved to the United States because his driver's license was revoked in his own country.

CABLE TV SERVICE REPRESENTATIVE
-The only career available for those people actually deemed too slow to work as Post Office Clerks.

CAR SALESMAN
-Caution: Recent public opinion polls rate "Car Salesman" one step below "Car *Thief.*"

CARNIVAL RIDE OPERATOR
-To be seriously considered here, an applicant should have at least nine teeth missing. Extra points are given to those with no teeth up front.

CARNIVAL RIDE OPERATOR AT DISNEY WORLD
-A Carnival Ride Operator with dentures.

CARPENTER
-We've Only Just Begun considering the job possibilities, but if you want to be on Top Of The World, a Superstar, where all your people long to be Close To You, while bringing back the fun from Yesterday Once More, just remember that It's Going To Take Some Time.

CARTOGRAPHER (MAP DRAWER)
-This is a job that's pretty much already done. A map of Iowa is a map of Iowa. Unless there's some major shifting in the Earth, you're going to spend a lot of time in the unemployment line.

CARTOONIST/ANIMATOR/ILLUSTRATOR
-Your primary task involves bringing life to a work. For instance, what would this book be if an Illustrator hadn't been hired? (Probably a buck cheaper.)

CASHIER
-This job has changed in recent years. You used to have to take an item, read the price tag, and ring it up manually. Nowadays, all you do is take an item, run it by a laser beam, run it by again, try it a third time, and then read the price tag and ring it up manually.

CEMENT TRUCK DRIVER
-Big-time responsibility. When warnings on medicine labels say one shouldn't operate heavy machinery, **you're** the guy they're talking about.

CENSOR
-Censors have got to be the most f*@^*@ #/^! people on earth.

CENSUS TAKER
-You should have a large savings account. Nine-year periods of unemployment are common.

CERTIFIED PUBLIC ACCOUNTANT
-A person who prefers bonds to blondes.

CHAUFFEUR
-This is a person who drives a brand new $100,000 limo during working hours, and a 1973 Gremlin home.

CHEF
-If you saw this guy on the street, you'd shudder at the thought of him touching your food. But because he wears a tall hat, it's OK.

CHESS PLAYER
-Sit on your butt, move little horses around a board, and try to look clever. Yep—sounds like a real job to me.

CHIEF EXECUTIVE OFFICER
-The CEO is often the person who, years ago, began working in the mail room, struggling to climb the ladder, and finally, after countless days and nights of nonstop labor, quit his job and went to work for Dad.

CHIEF OPERATING OFFICER
-The Chief Operating Officer is often the person who, years ago, began working in the mail room...steaming open important-looking letters, learning inside secrets, and then used them to cheat his way to the top.

CHOREOGRAPHER
-If you can say the words, "C'mon everybody...five, six, seven, eight!..." while simultaneously maintaining a lisp and a feeling of sheer intensity, you've found your profession.

CHRISTMAS TREE SALESPERSON
-Not a bad job, unless you like taking your annual vacation in December.

CIA AGENT
(Unable to disclose at this time)

CIVIL ENGINEER
1) A person who meticulously designs roads and bridges so these structures will begin to develop dangerous cracks within six months after being completed.
2) An Engineer who doesn't believe in violence.

CLARINETIST
-How many occupations enable you to make money simply by putting your lips around an instrument? (This is just a hypothetical question.)

CLOTHING INSPECTOR
-A highly competitive field. Senior Inspectors (#1 - #5) make double that of Junior Inspectors (#6 - #10). Trainees (greater than #10) are paid only in the form of defective pieces of clothing.

CLOWN
-Any occupation that makes people laugh at you is very special. Just ask an Encyclopedia Salesman.

COBBLER
-A somewhat confusing trade, in that you will either:

A) fix shoes;

B) be an iced beverage containing wine; or

C) take the form of a deep-dish fruit pie.

COLLEGE DEAN
-This is the person you complain to about a bad Professor, right before finding out the Professor and Dean are best friends.

COLLEGE PLACEMENT ADVISOR
-In this capacity, you will help business and engineering students find well-paying jobs. As for the rest of the student body, they might as well become College Placement Advisors.

COLLEGE PROFESSOR
-In order to really look like a Professor, as opposed to just a Teacher, a beard is strongly recommended — even for women.

COMEDIAN
-As a professional Comedian, you can achieve the ultimate revenge: show up at your old high school and approach Miss Grumpster, who repeatedly asked you how you intend to make a living with your smart mouth. Let her know that you've now **succeeded** in making a living with your smart mouth, and that you make in thirty minutes what she makes in a month.

COMPTROLLER
-Not a position for the wild and crazy. In fact, the key here is appearing to be in a constant state of valium-induced restraint. If you ever get the urge to, say, get a triple scoop of Ben & Jerry's **Chunky Monkey**, a career change is in order.

COMPUTER CONSULTANT
-In this field, you will spend countless hours tinkering with O.P.W. (Other People's Wangs). Hey—whatever makes your floppy hard.

COMPUTER PROGRAMMER
-Victims of high school bullies can get revenge by becoming Computer Programmers. As a Programmer, you can hack your way into the lives of everyone you've ever hated, ruining their credit rating and shutting off their utilities and phone service. Who said life isn't fair?

COMPUTER REPAIRMAN
-The computer revolution took off without training enough Computer Repairmen. Now you can attend Comp-U-School Institute and graduate into this exciting and rewarding profession. And even if you can't find employment after shelling out thousands of dollars, at least you'll walk away with your own set of tools.

CONDUCTOR, ORCHESTRA
-This occupation has just three requirements: a thorough knowledge of music, an intricate sense of timing, and a real bad haircut.

CONGRESSMAN
-A person who is overpaid to tell us how money is being wasted.

CONSTRUCTION WORKER
-If the only nails you ever hit with a hammer are your *finger* nails, consider another field.

CONTORTIONIST
-Waking up in the morning will be nothing. Getting untangled and out of bed is a different story.

CONTRACTOR, CONSTRUCTION
-It's your duty to make sure all the workers on a job are qualified to read blueprints, stand on narrow beams, and whistle at hot babes walking by.

CONVENIENCE STORE CLERK
-Despite popular belief, this job does not require you to be of Iranian or Indian descent. However, the job application forms are only available in those languages.

CONVENIENCE STORE CLERK, NIGHT SHIFT
-This line of work involves being held up at gunpoint at least once each shift, and occasionally ringing up a purchase.

COOK
-A Chef who can't balance a tall hat on his head.

COPY MACHINE REPAIRMAN
-This individual is easy to spot, in that he shows up at your office more often than most employees.

COPYWRITER, DIRECT MAIL
-You will **attempt** to CATCH PEOPLE'S EYES in:
- Letters

- Brochures

- Junk Mail

by using CAPITAL LETTERS, <u>underlining</u>, and
- dashes - for no grammatical reasons.

   P.S. You'll use lots of P.S.'s too.

CORONER
-It's your job to figure out the cause of mysterious deaths. For instance, if a dead body has several extra holes in it, and there's a gun on the floor nearby, you'd assume either A) He's been shot; or B) He had a penchant for dressing like a piece of swiss cheese, but nobody accepted this peculiarity, so he decided to ingest an entire bottle of aspirin to kill himself, but couldn't get the childproof cap off with his hands, so he took out his gun and shot the top of the bottle off and then downed the pills and died.

COSMETOLOGIST
-Your job is to show a woman how a different combination of make-up can change her entire look. (The fact that her first stop after leaving you is the nearest bathroom so she can wash it all off before anyone sees her isn't your problem.)

COURIER/FEDERAL EXPRESS DRIVER
-Spend enough years in this capacity, learning to drive faster every day, and you'll soon become eligible to become a Pizza Delivery Person!

COVER GIRL
-A woman without pores.

CRANE OPERATOR
-If Freud were alive today, he would recommend this job as the ultimate psychological lift for a man with a low sexual self-image.

CRISIS HOT LINE VOLUNTEER
-Do you get stressed out when the car in front of you is ONLY doing the speed limit? If so, you may not be the pressure-resistant person this job requires.

CRITIC (ENTERTAINMENT)
-If you have no actual talents of your own and you're damn angry about it, become a Critic and try to convince the public that it's not just you— **nobody** has talent. On a scale of 1-5, this job gets: NO STARS.

CROSSWALK GUARD
-This is a very important occupation, often handled by retired folks who have trouble seeing their bran in the morning, much less a car barreling down the street. The point of their employment here is to teach children they must look out for themselves when crossing a street.

CURATOR
-If you're one of those people who never throws anything away, and you therefore have a garage and closets full of junk you "may need someday," you'll feel right at home in this area.

CUSTOMS INSPECTOR
-This is the person who asks visitors if they're carrying any illegal drugs. Those people who are inane enough to answer "Yes" go to jail, and upon release, become Customs Inspectors.

ANCER

-Here's one profession where if you're not wonderful, you're awful. A Dancer who's just a little bit off can make Swan Lake look like **The Benny Hill Show.**

DAY CARE OPERATOR
-If, when you're on a plane, you prefer crying babies be put in the overhead compartment, this job's not for you.

DEMOLITION EXPERT
-Remember when you were a kid, and you got in trouble for destroying a toy, or a piece of furniture, or the house? Here, you can do it every day, on a **huge** scale, and no one's going to yell at you! (Unless you accidentally implode the wrong building.)

DENTAL HYGIENIST
-The only job officially listed by the Department of Labor which requires that you ask people to spit.

DENTIST
-How can your sadistic tendencies make you rich? "Open wide."

DEPT. OF MOTOR VEHICLES WORKER
-Your job is to stand behind the counter and help people as slowly as possible, thereby serving as a constant reminder from the State Transportation Office to **Slow Down.**

DETECTIVE
-Get used to being called a Private Eye, a Sleuth, a Gumshoe, an Undercover Man, a Shadow, a Spy, a Plainclothesman, an Investigator, a Dick, an Operative, a Fed, a Police Officer, or an Agent. Some of the people you catch may even call you a few other names.

DIRECTOR, TV/FILM
-Hired by a Producer, this individual takes the words of a great writer, and the talent of great actors, and screws it all up for the screen.

DIRECTORY ASSISTANCE OPERATOR
-To be good at this job, you must sound fed up with every person who calls. With the right intonation of the words, "What city?" and "Yes?", you can actually make a caller feel guilty for bothering you.

DISC JOCKEY
-During at least one job in your career, you must pretend to like Barry Manilow.

DISC JOCKEY, JAZZ/OVERNIGHT SHIFT
-To be a true late night jazz D.J., you must put special emphasis on details.... "That was **Birdland** by Maynard Ferguson, Joe Tweddle on trombone, Bill Parsons on sax, Art Jones on drums. The recording was made on June 13th, 1966 at the Mid-town Theater in New York City. Joe was wearing a green turtleneck sweater with a small stain on the left sleeve. Bill had just had a fight with his mother-in-law, Helen. Art had some food caught in his teeth from dinner that night. He had a cheeseburger. It was well-done...."

DISHWASHER
-Never choose an occupation that a major appliance can handle.

DOCTOR
-You'll spend 80 hours a week, 52 weeks a year, for multiple years, studying, sweating, and learning everything about the human body, so years from now, when your trusting patient asks what's wrong with him, you can confidently say, "Geez, it could be a lot of things. It's hard to tell for sure."

DOG OBEDIENCE INSTRUCTOR

-Here's the ideal employment opportunity for the person who has the desire to be "in charge," but realizes that no human being in their right mind would ever listen to him.

DOG WALKER

-This can be a depressing business, when you realize the poodle you're walking probably has a larger inheritance than you do.

DOOR-TO-DOOR SALESMAN

-This field involves shlepping around a cumbersome array of useless products, in an attempt to annoy every person ever born. After being told several thousand times "where to go," these people often go find religion, and three months later, they're waking you up Saturday morning to offer you free pamphlets.

DRAG RACER

-If you think your auto insurance is high *now*, just wait until your agent finds out your car goes from zero to 200 m.p.h. in 6.3 seconds.

DRAWBRIDGE OPERATOR

-Up & Down. Up & Down. All day & all night long. Your sex life should be so good.

DRIVING SCHOOL INSTRUCTOR

-Considering the drivers we see out on the road today, it's obvious that the ad for this job reads "No experience necessary."

DRUGGIST

-The answer for those who couldn't quite get themselves to "Just Say No." As an official drug dispenser, you can use your own body as a test site and see what really happens when taking a big orange pill and a little purple pill at the same time.

CONOMIST

-A person who is interviewed for his expert economic opinions. In the rare instance that one of his theories is correct, you can usually turn the channel to see another Economist asserting the exact opposite theory.

EDITOR, LITERARY
-This profession involves telling a writer what to write, what not to write, how to write, when to write, who to write, why to write, and so on....If this sounds interesting to you, why not just knock out the middleman and become a Writer....

EDITOR, FILM
-(Sorry—In an attempt to keep the book moving, this job description was left on the publishing house floor.)

ELECTRICIAN
-This is one of those jobs where if you're not good at your craft, you may not be around to get better.

ELECTROENCEPHALOGRAPHIC TECHNOLOGIST
-Your business card will have to be the size of a diving board.

ELEVATOR OPERATOR
-The job certainly has its ups and downs. (OK, so it's an elementary pun. What do you want for a few bucks— Shakespeare?))

ELVIS IMPERSONATOR
-This vocation may soon be eliminated if the continued sightings of Elvis prove to be true. Apparently, Elvis has not only left the building, he's left the graveyard.
Thnkyuvrymch.

EMBALMER
-The answer for those who failed Cosmetology School.

ENCYCLOPEDIA SALESPERSON
-A person who has a vast array of knowledge at his fingertips, except the knowledge that nobody wants to buy encyclopedia sets.

ENGINEER
-A sad career mistake for those who realize, 3 1/2 years into college, that their profession actually has nothing to do with choo-choo trains.

ENGINEER
(THE KIND WHO <u>DOESN'T</u> DRIVE A TRAIN)
-Armed with a calculator, thick glasses, and shirt pocket protector, these geeks couldn't pick up a Call Girl at a Eunuchs' Convention.

ENTREPRENEUR
-This person throws away a steady paycheck in order to bring his or her lifelong dream to fruition. After approximately five months of trying to pay the rent and the Visa bills, said person can usually be seen on their knees, begging for a return to that steady paycheck.

ESCALATOR OPERATOR
-Just checking to see if you're paying attention.

EXORCIST
-The only occupation in which the IRS actually allows you to write off a goat's pancreas.

EXPERT (ANY SUBJECT)
-A person who knows nothing more than you or me, but gets paid big bucks to **sound** like he does.

EX-PRESIDENT
-Any career that offers ongoing Secret Service protection for your dog can't be all bad.

EXTERMINATOR
-A hired entomological hit man, who is forced to drive around with a 7-foot fiberglass cockroach on his roof. Counseling is often required in later years.

EXTRA, TV/MOVIE
-As an Extra, your duties consist of waiting twelve hours to be filmed, and then walking in front of the camera in just the right way so that nobody in the audience will notice you.

AA INVESTIGATOR

-You've got to be a pretty sick puppy to sit by the phone, waiting for a call to go sift through the wreckage of an airplane crash. After a few years, you may want to curl up in your own little black box.

FARMER
-The Farmer is the Backbone of America. After all, where would we be without Farmer's Daughter jokes?

FASHION DESIGNER
-A person who makes large sums of money by declaring that everything in your closet is now out of style, while proclaiming that her new line of thousand-dollar elephant suits is currently what's "in."

FBI AGENT
-If you like wearing Hawaiian shirts, if you're into scat singing, or if **Animal House** was your fave movie of all time, you're probably not what the FBI is looking for.

FEMALE IMPERSONATOR
1) With incredible makeup and lavish outfits, you will appear to the audience to actually be a woman. Your job is to be so convincing that male

viewers, upon finding out you're truly a man, will sustain serious psychosexual self-doubts.
2) Tyne Daley

FINANCIAL PLANNER
-The very nature of this business dictates that the Financial Planner not be very good. Otherwise, he'd already be in Acapulco sipping frozen strawberry daiquiris.

FIREFIGHTER
-Your job entails being awakened at 4 a.m. to hose down a mobile home where some idiot had a lit cigarette in bed. You better have a very forgiving personality.

FLIGHT ATTENDANT
-Air travelers often have some apprehension while sitting in a multi-ton metal tube that's hurling through the air at a high rate of speed without a guy wire or even a net. It's your job to soothe those passengers by making sure each is given a foil bag containing four peanuts.

FLOOR MANAGER
-Unless you're having a new one installed, or you're experiencing a major earthquake, most floors just don't need managing.

FLORIST
-People will visit your shop at the happiest times of their lives, the saddest times, and when they're just trying to get lucky. In these times of drastically unclear thinking, it's your job to convince them that they should shell out 65 bucks for some flowers that grow in the ground for free.

FOOTBALL COACH
-A guy whose blood pressure is inversely proportional to his win-loss record.

FOOTBALL QUARTERBACK
-This is the only occupation (other than that of Tailor) in today's society where it's perfectly acceptable for a man to put his hands in another man's crotch.

FOREST RANGER
-If **Smokey the Bear** meant a lot to you as a kid and still holds a special place in your heart, you should become a Forest Ranger. In fact, on slow nights, you can even put on a **Smokey** costume and terrorize campers.

FUNERAL DIRECTOR
-The only occupation starting with the letters F-U-N. Of course, if you're a morbid kind of person, this job **could** be fun.

"Ever get that *gnawing* feeling something bad's about to happen?"

**AMBLER**

1) To determine your chances of winning at any given game, you will factor in statistical formulas, possible outcomes, and prior experience. You will then ignore all of this information and play until you're out of money.
2) Police Explosives Defuser

GAME SHOW HOST
-A man with lots of hair, lots of teeth, and no discernible talents.

GAME SHOW PRIZE STROKER
-A good-looking gal with a big smile, a truck-load of hairspray, and the talent to look excited over a lifetime supply of Rice-a-Roni.

GARBAGE COLLECTOR
-Rarely-mentioned benefits include "All You Can Eat!"

GAS STATION ATTENDANT
-A guy who couldn't master the phrase, "Do ya want fries with that?"

GENETICIST
-A person who spends his time working on designer genes.

GLASS EATER
-There's not much of a demand for this these days, but remember what your parents always said— Nobody ever made it big by giving up.

GOFER
-While you'll certainly be a big help to the people above you, you'll be thought of as one step below your rodent friend of the same name.

GOLFER
-If you've always wanted to be a sports professional, but your athletic abilities were about equivalent to a high wire walker with vertigo, gather your balls, grab your putter, and yell **Fore**!

GOLF SPORTSCASTER
-A job where laryngitis is not a valid excuse to call in sick.

GOVERNMENT WORKER
-A smart career move, in that your job is fairly secure. (Unless, of course, you foolishly break the rules and become productive.)

GRAVE DIGGER
-Remember when your pet hamster died, and you buried him in the side yard? Think of this job as hamster disposal, taken to a much higher level. Of course, if you also flushed your dead goldfish down the toilet, you may be more inclined to work with burials at sea.

GREETER
-Picture Rip Taylor on speed.

GREETING CARD WRITER
-A wonderful job, writing lines about Cupid, you'll be a success, as long as they're stupid.

GRUNT (CABLE SPLICER)
-Before becoming a Grunt, please consider that the following phrase has never, ever, been uttered in history: "Mom and Dad, I've met the man of my dreams. He's a Grunt."

GURU
-A bad career move, simply because every time you talk to your Mom, you'll have to endure, "Oh, of course Mr. Know-it-all, Mr. Smarty-pants...."

GYMNAST
-Dressing in skimpy outfits and bending your body in wild ways in front of total strangers...sounds like early training for a Porn Star.

GYNECOLOGIST
-A good alternative for lonely Dentists, in that the jobs are basically identical. "Open... This won't hurt a bit... I'm sorry, Did that hurt?... You can spit out now." OK, maybe not *identical.*

HAIR STYLIST
-If you've always felt like you should be a Choreographer, but just never liked that whole Dance thing, here's a good alternative.

HANDYMAN
-Not as simple as it used to be. Today, to really get anywhere as a Handyman, you must first have at least a Bachelor's degree in Handology.

HAZARDOUS WASTE WORKER
-Your major duty here involves the removal and safe disposal of 7-11 pastries after their expiration date.

HEATING/A.C. MECHANIC
-The good thing about this job is that when customers need you, they **really** need you. And they'll pay **anything** for a repair. And you can become **rich**.

HELICOPTER TRAFFIC REPORTER
-This airborne specialty lets you get back at any injustices the world has inflicted upon you. Your job is to direct thousands of helpless drivers into bumper-to-bumper traffic, then piss them off by flying over

them at 90 miles per hour, informing them they're stuck in bumper-to-bumper traffic.

HELPER
-A Gofer without a title. The main purpose of a Helper is to remind the Boss that if he wants something done right, he has to do it himself.

HISTORIAN
-If you've ever uttered something like, "Back when I was in school, we didn't have calculators...we didn't have desks...we didn't have teachers...", you are a Historian.

HOCKEY PLAYER
-An occupation that the school bully can shoot for.

HOMEMAKER
-This person is in charge of running everything in the household. With no co-workers to cover for you, you have one of those few jobs where you actually have to **work**.

HOME SHOPPING NETWORK HOSTESS
-The Answer to the Question: "What do high school cheerleaders become when/if they graduate?"

HORTICULTURIST
-Schooling for this occupation requires the taking of a foreign language.... **Very** foreign. OK, **Plant Talk**. The final exam measures your ability to fluently converse with a begonia.

HOTEL DESK CLERK
-A person whose ability to locate one's reservations are amazingly improved by the sight of Andrew Jackson in green.

HOUSEKEEPER
-Divorce a celebrity, and you too can become a "Housekeeper."

HOUSE SITTER
1) Your job consists of staying in a person's house and making sure nothing goes wrong. Unfortunately, a few little fires can ruin your whole career.
2) Couch Potato

HOUSEWIFE/HOUSEHUSBAND
-Here, you will take care of household and family obligations while your spouse works outside the home. As your partner will occasionally be unappreciative of the work you do, a month-long strike on your part will usually snap them back to reality.

HURRICANE SPECIALIST

-A great position for a sadistic person. The only time your job gets exciting is when lives and property are seriously threatened.

ICE CREAM TRUCK DRIVER
-Considering you have to listen to whiny music, clanging bells, and screaming brats all day, wouldn't you really rather be unemployed?

INSURANCE SALESPERSON
-It's this guy's job to give you the assurance that no matter what tragedy could possibly occur, it couldn't be as bad as your appointment with him.

INTERIOR DECORATOR
-If, in your college dorm room, you built shelves using wood on stacks of cinder blocks, you're probably not what this field is looking for. However, if the phrase, "Oh, those curtains have just got to go!" rolls easily off your tongue, get out that ruler.

INTERN
-This is generally a young person who assists those in broadcasting, medicine, or government with simple errands, chores, and sexual favors.

INTERPRETER
-A fun job. Here, you can suggest a romantic interlude, insult a world leader, and basically change the course of history just by making up what the other person supposedly said.

INVENTOR
-If your workshop is overflowing with lots of real technical-looking gadgets that have yet to do a damn thing, you're a certified would-be Inventor.

INVESTIGATOR
-If you can figure out what the hell happened to Richie's older brother on the TV show **Happy Days** back in the mid-70's, you're definitely qualified to be an Investigator.

IRS AGENT
-Everyone will hate you. Even if they are perfect citizens and receive five-figure refunds, they will hate you. Even your Mom will hate you. I don't even know you, and *I* hate you.

JANITOR

-The ideal job for corporate espionage. In this position, you can sift through the trash, gather all of the company's vital strategic information, and then open your own competing firm. With your "insider" knowledge, your ex-company will soon go under, and then you can hire your ex-boss as your Janitor.

JEWELER

-The field of Acting comes in handy here. You must convince the customer that a tiny piece of rock, which has no actual uses, is worth thousands of dollars. If you start laughing, it ruins the whole pitch.

JUDGE

-In this role, you will make important decisions which affect many lives on a daily basis. As a rule of thumb, if you have trouble with life's simpler decisions, such as what toppings to get on your pizza, don't become a Judge.

KENNEL OPERATOR

-You will be surrounded by loud, yelping, whining, barking dogs all day long. But don't worry—just keep thinking that when you get home, you can relax, put your feet up, and turn on the TV to watch old reruns of **Lassie**.

KINDERGARTEN TEACHER

-You're the bridge between nursery school and first grade. You're therefore the person who has to break the news to all those kids that their daily routine over the next dozen or so years won't actually consist of Simon Says, finger painting, and Duck Duck Goose.

KKK GRAND WIZARD

-You must be a self-motivator, in that this job usually isn't represented at a school's Career Day. A history of mental illness is a definite plus.

LABOR MEDIATOR

-If you thrive on disagreement... if your best memories of childhood are those of your parents arguing over the position of the toilet seat... if you hang around customer complaint counters just for the excitement—sign up for this occupation today, and you can personally deal with pissed-off people constantly!

LABORATORY TECHNICIAN

-So you like the medical field, but you don't see yourself as a Doctor. Become a Lab Technician! While working in the lab isn't as exciting as in the **Frankenstein** movies, it still beats shaving a guy for surgery.

LANDSCAPE ARTIST

-Your job is to take dirt, shrubs, and rocks, and spread them around an area which, for building purposes, was just cleared of dirt, shrubs, and rocks.

LAND SURVEYOR

-Here's the ideal job for peeping Toms. You didn't think those little telescopes were really focused on the street, did you?

LANDLORD
-What a powerful title! **Landlord**....Lord of the Land! Who'd imagine this high and mighty being would be required to fix Mrs. Scragman's broken toilet at 3 a.m.

LAUNDRY WORKER
1) *(See Spot) (See Spot Run)*
2) When customers hand you their claim ticket, it is your responsibility to make it look like you can't find their garment. Once they are in a state of panic, you can then "find" the piece of clothing. By this time, the customer is usually so happy to have their garment back, they won't even notice that you made the spot worse.

LAWYER
1) An individual who can't pronounce the word **scruples.**
2) A profession which wouldn't exist had there been a few more commandments.
3) The only person who adult vultures teach their young to fear.
4) The best evidence that God has a sense of humor.

LETTER CARRIER
-Through rain, sleet, snow, and minor hemorrhoidal irritation, your job is to bend, tear, mutilate, and lose every person's mail.

LIBRARIAN
-In this occupation, it's your job to keep everyone in the library quiet, while you proceed to speak as loudly as you damn please. (Warning: After 5 years on the job, the Library of Congress insists you wear those half-moon glasses at the end of your nose and put your hair up in a bun. Even if you're a man.)

LIFE INSURANCE SALESPERSON
-A tough way to earn a living. You must sell your customer on the fact that in order for him to collect anything, he has to die first.

LINGUIST
-A person who can sound good ordering food at any restaurant in EPCOT.

LION TAMER
-You're mistakenly thinking **you're** the one with nine lives.

LITIGATOR
1) If you've always wanted to be like Perry Mason and make the prime suspect break down on the stand and admit to the murder, don't be a Litigator—it just doesn't happen that way in real life. Of course, if you're **really** into the show, you as the attorney could always break down in the

courtroom and admit to committing the murder. That would beat any Perry Mason episode.
2) A short person at the University of Florida.

LOAN OFFICER
-Here, if you determine that a young couple does indeed need money, it's your obligation to crush their dreams and smother their future. What could be more fun?

LUMBERJACK
-If your idea of a fulfilling day at work involves a lengthy discussion between you and your work mates about your favorite ballet stars, you'd be smart to rule out this occupation.

MACHINIST
-You are the beginning of a vicious cycle of greed. You take a raw material worth, lets say, ten cents.... Make it into some useful product worth, lets say, one dollar....The product is then shipped to a distributor where it's sold to the retail market for, lets say, ten dollars....The retail store then sells it to the public for a special sale price (This week only!) of $49.95... which, lets say, is a complete rip-off. Let's just say you started the whole thing—It is, therefore, all your fault.

MAGICIAN
-The idea here is to keep a smile on your face while you fool people. The best part is, if you ever decide to change careers, you can use the same skills to become a Politician.

MAID
-This individual has the privilege of being the only person to see what a pig you really are. (Unless you're one of those really weird people who cleans up before the Maid arrives.)

MAIL ROOM WORKER
-The perfect occupation for those who are too lethargic to work a *real* job, yet too energetic to work for the Department of Motor Vehicles.

MAKE-UP ARTIST, DEPARTMENT STORE
-As you might've guessed by looking at these ladies, this job requires you to wear a sampling of EVERY make-up item in your display case simultaneously.

MANAGEMENT TRAINEE
-In this position, you'll learn exactly how long to submerge the fries for perfect crispness.

MANAGER
-Put in long hours at work, every day for lots of years, and chances are, someday...you'll be laid off. If you've got the initiative and drive to become a Manager, you might as well quit working for some bozo and start your own company.

MANICURIST
-You'll spend your life having people give you the finger.

MARINE BIOLOGIST
1) You will attempt to study underwater animal and plant life. Unfortunately, you will end up doing most of your work on land, since desk-top computers tend to short out rather quickly once submerged.
2) A scientist who studies the life of a U.S. Marine.

MARKET RESEARCHER
-This very intriguing occupation leads you to ask total strangers questions like, "Do you prefer plain or floral-patterned toilet paper?" The answer will help you decide something like the name of a new automobile.

MASSEUSE
-If you go around squeezing the bodies of strangers, you're arrested. If you get paid for it, you're a **Masseuse.**

MATHEMATICIAN
-The life of any party. "Hey Bob! Why didn't the square root of 169 multiply?... Cause you can't divide by zero!!" Nonstop laughter.

MEAT CUTTER
-The hell with evolution. Do what you do best.

MECHANIC, AUTO
-If you can say phrases like, "I found another 'big' problem while I was in there" with a straight face, you can earn big bucks here.

MECHANICAL ARTIST (DRAFTSMAN)
-Many in this field had originally wanted to become famous cartoonists, like Peanuts' creator Charles Shultz, but just didn't have the talent. Now, sadly, they suffer from Peanuts envy.

MEDICAL INTERN
-In this position, you get to wear a stethoscope and one of those official-looking white coats. Of course, you don't **have** to be in the medical profession to wear a stethoscope and white coat, but you may look a bit odd if you do and you're, say, a Construction Worker.

MEDIUM
-A person who helps contact and communicate with the world of the deceased. If you're the only one in your area, you'll be known as a Medium-rare.

METEOROLOGIST
-If you can look at a radar screen and honestly tell the difference between clouds and ground clutter, look into this profession.

MICROBIOLOGIST
-A field of biology to consider if you are under 5'2".

MIDWIFE
-This role used to involve helping a woman give birth. Today, however, "Helping a woman give birth" could mean being a surrogate and actually **giving** birth to the woman's baby. Before signing up, read the fine print!

MIND READER
-The cardinal rule to remember about Mind Readers: Their abilities are inversely proportional to the amount of attention they seek.

MINER
-This job can satisfy the kid in you. You get to ride on a little train into a dark cave wearing a hat with a bright light on it. (Keep in mind, however, that child labor laws often prevent Miners from working full-time jobs.)

MINISTER
-People will turn to you for guidance, often at life's most trying times. Depending on what type of mood you're in that day, you can either help them, or you can tell them you've got your own problems and to go write Ann Landers.

MISSIONARY
-To a lay person, this is a notable position.

MODEL
-Very good looks and an SAT score below 7 indicate this is your type of employment. (**Hint:** If you were able to read the word **Model** above, you're too intelligent to qualify. A Model's intellectual capacity is usually limited to 3-letter words (such as "BMW"), or 5-word sentences (like "Are you rich and famous?").)

MODEL, BEFORE
-Considering the fact that you are demonstrating to the world your "lack of physical attributes," you either:

1) have an incredibly-high degree of self-confidence;
2) are a true masochist; or
3) have to pay the rent.

MORTICIAN
-An important prerequisite to this field is the ability to control one's urge to laugh at inappropriate times.

MOVER
-Kind of an advanced position for postal letter carriers. Here, you get to damage, mutilate, and lose **whole pieces of furniture!**

MOVIE STAR
-A person whose relative was in the right place at the right time.

MOVIE THEATER CONCESSION STAND WORKER
-One of life's ironic coincidences, in that a product in the counter is called "Goobers," and the guys **behind** the counter are called "Goobers."

MOVIE THEATER TICKET TEARER
-This is the perfect career if you want to tell your friends across the country that you are in the movie business.

MUSICIAN
-Here, you create sounds by using your body and an instrument. If you don't use the instrument, you're either a Singer, or you're disgusting.

ANNY

Large men named Bubba may have trouble finding employment in this capacity.

NEWS REPORTER
-This communications specialist must be skilled enough to shove a microphone in the face of someone who has just experienced a horrendous personal tragedy, and ask, "How do you feel?"

NUCLEAR PHYSICIST
-Be prepared for... "Yeah, and I'm the President of the United States. Why don't you go hang out with your friend over there, the Brain Surgeon."

NUCLEAR POWER PLANT WORKER
-Perfect if you're suicidal, but you want to take your time about it.

NUN
-If you're enjoying reading through a book like this, you're just *not* Nun material.

NURSE
-Picture being the servant, maid, and caretaker to dozens of ill people, being ultimately responsible for them, getting harassed by their families and doctors, risking your own health, and getting a disgustingly-low income in return for it all. (Go to school a few more years and become a Doctor.)

NURSERY SCHOOL TEACHER
-In this profession, you will often provide the only guidance and shaping a young person receives. You can therefore do fun experiments like raising a whole class to sound like Charles Nelson Reilly.

NUTRITIONIST
-It's easy to spot a Nutritionist at a party. He's the sickly- looking one near the food who's munching on the dining room table.

OCEANOGRAPHER
-If you think **plankton** is what the Dentist scrapes off your teeth, this field isn't for you.

OIL RIG WORKER
-If you love playing your tape of **La Cage Aux Folles** loudly every night, you probably won't fit in here.

OPERATOR
-You may develop low self-esteem here, because nobody will ever call you just to talk. All they'll do is **want** things from you. "Connect my call. Dial this number. Get the police." Who needs these pests?

OPHTHALMOLOGIST
-If you can spell the name of this profession, you'd probably do better as an English Teacher.

OPTICIAN
-It's your job to help fit people with corrective eye wear, and to try to unload those striped, octagon-shaped frames that have been sitting on the shelf since the disco era.

OPTOMETRIST

-To find out if you're right for this career, cover your right eye and read this. Now cover your left eye and read this. Now cover both eyes and read this. If you can, **See Psychic.**

ORTHODONTIST

-A rather crude profession, in that with today's medical technology, your job is to improve a person's bite by strapping heavy-duty wires across their teeth, and painfully applying countless tons of pressure. You're kind of like Satan's rep on Earth.

AGE

-77.

PAGE, STUDIO
-In an attempt to get into show business, you will do work far below your intellectual capacity and be treated like dirt. But in the long run, it could all pay off if you happen to pass by Ruth Buzzi in the hallway.

PAINTER, ARTISTIC
-If your art skills today aren't noticeably different than they were in your 2nd grade Art Class, your works will either be laughed at, or they'll fetch millions of dollars. No telling which.

PAINTER, HOUSE
-While this job is not as prestigious as its artistic counterpart, at least this one lets you buy life's little extras, like food.

PARAMEDIC
-An ideal career for the serious rubbernecker.

PARENT, FULL-TIME
-This round-the-clock job rarely gets the respect or financial compensation it deserves. On the other hand, you don't have Mr. Sternhound breathing down your neck, waiting to reprimand you if you take a moment to sneeze.

PARK RANGER
-One of the few careers left that lets you wear a wacky hat on days other than October 31.

PARKING CITATION OFFICER
-In this position, you will be trained to arrive at a car right after the meter runs out, and right before the car's owner shows up, thus leaving you just enough time to accomplish your duty — ruining a person's day and making life on Earth worse for the entire human race.

PARTY PLANNER
-Warning:
Stopping by 7-11 for a bag of chips and a six-pack doesn't exactly qualify you for this business.

PEACE CORP VOLUNTEER
-A role for the true humanitarian. You won't be invited to fancy luncheons. Your picture won't appear on the society page. And you won't have luxuries like electricity and running water. On the

other hand, where else can you get to know 59 varieties of mosquitoes intimately?

PEDODONTIST
-If we were to follow the laws of prefixes and suffixes, this profession either works with children's teeth, or helps people who put their foot in their mouth.

PERSONAL SERVANT
-If you're employed in this capacity by a celebrity, you'll never again have to rely on those trashy tabloids for your gossip. In fact, you can even moonlight as an official "Source Close To."

PERSONNEL WORKER
-Never take a job where you might someday have to type up your own pink slip.

PET GROOMER
-The answer for those who fail Cosmetology School, but aren't into embalming.

PET PSYCHOLOGIST
-In Beverly Hills, you can actually make a good living talking to a dachshund. Is this a great planet, or what?

PHARMACIST
-If you've ever wondered what happened to the mindless druggies of the 60's, they've now opened their own shops and call themselves Pharmacists.

PHILANTHROPIST
-In this capacity, you give money to others. Kind of the opposite of a Televangelist.

PHOTO LAB WORKER
-The ultimate position for anyone looking to get rich. Here, you get to see who in town is really kinky, and then blackmail them.

PHOTOGRAPHER
-With modern cameras being fully-automated right down to the focus, a chimpanzee could handle this job. Of course, if you want **good** photos, you'd need a **creative** chimpanzee.

PHYS ED TEACHER
-If you:

A) enjoy wearing shorts in an educational setting;
B) had trouble making it though your **own** educational setting; and
C) can't spell the words **educational** or **setting**, you've found your calling.

"Side effects? Don't worry,
I take 'em myself, everyday!"

PIANO SALESPERSON
-While not a bad occupation, the door-to-door route can be pure hell.

PIANO TEACHER
-This is an extremely grand undertaking, considering you're trying to teach an inanimate object.

PIANO TUNER
-While your career will B-flat, you may C-sharp visions of yourself changing careers and entering the military to become A-major.

PIZZA DELIVERY PERSON
-The perfect job for the frustrated individual who couldn't cut it as a Race Car Driver.

PLASTIC SURGEON, BREAST ENHANCEMENT
1) After enough years, your profession will be responsible for making every small-breasted woman larger and every large-breasted woman smaller, so that eventually, bras will only need to come in one size.
2) A Doctor who puts on a good front.

PLASTIC SURGEON, NOSE JOBS
-The only business where you can advertise, "Come on in and pick your nose!"

PLUMBER
-This is a good career if you'd like to make the money a Lawyer does, but you don't want to be embarrassed when someone asks you what you do.

PLUMBER, BROOKLYN
-The only occupation where a guy can make forty-five bucks an hour by saying things like "Dis here pipe's gotta go... We here's gonna have ta tear out da whole flaw."

PODIATRIST
-Stay away from this area unless you clearly have an uncontrollable foot fetish. Otherwise, you'll never really be able to enjoy those lunchtime corn chips after touching old Mrs. Langford's bunions.

POLICE BOMB SQUAD MEMBER
-A good way for convicted criminals to do their community service.

POLICE OFFICER
-Not the best of jobs, in that you put your life on the line every day, yet pull in less annual income than the average criminal you're chasing.

POLICE SKETCH ARTIST
-Wanna be a cop, but you're a little too wimpy? Have difficulty supporting the weight of a gun belt? Enjoy showing crime victims a page of noses? If you answered **Yes** to all of the above, you were made for this occupation.

POLITICIAN
-A person who truly believes, despite massive opposition and indisputable proof, that he is not an idiot.

POSTAL CLERK
-If snails could stand behind a counter, hide their antennas, and yell "Next!", they'd not only fit in here—they'd put the current Postal Clerks out of business.
(Incidentally, this book was suppose to come out much earlier, but several months were spent standing in line at the Post Office waiting to mail the manuscript.)

POSTMAN
-You differ from Letter Carriers in that when you need a postal customer to sign for a package, you are required to ring the doorbell twice. Always.

PRESIDENT OF THE UNITED STATES
-The highest position a person without intelligence can attain.

PRIEST
-When a trusting soul comes to you and says, "Father, I have sinned," you must have the willpower to refrain from responses such as, "All *riiiight!* Let's hear all the sordid details! And don't leave anything out!"

PRINTER
1) Smelly inks and pungent chemicals will seep into your mucous membrane at least forty hours every week. After a few years, you will have a life-long buzz.
2) A person who dislikes cursive.

PRISON GUARD
-This is one occupation that makes the option of dealing with the **public** seem pretty good.

PROCTOLOGIST
-We all deal with them every day. You would just get paid for it.

PRODUCER, INDEPENDENT TV & FILM
-It is often asked what an Independent Producer does. It is often answered that he produces new business cards monthly.

PROFESSIONAL STUDENT
-The pay isn't great. In fact, it's almost as bad as being a Freelance Writer. But why enter the real world when Mom & Dad will keep shelling out the bucks for the classes you're supposed to be attending? (While you're **actually** learning exactly how many Budweisers it takes before you start seeing an image of Alexander Graham Bell wearing your sister's nightgown.)

PROOFREADER
-Research shows that persons in this position die early from heart problems, due to them seeing a final printed piece, and then spottting a typo.

PROSTHETICS MAKER
-Takes some getting used to, in that this is the only business where, if you accept credit cards, the **customers** can charge an arm and a leg.

PROSTITUTE
-The world's oldest profession, and still one of the most profitable. But make sure you either save a lot of money or have a back-up occupation for the later years—your income potential tends to sag as your body does.

PSYCHIATRIST
-This job involves asking people questions, pretending to be interested, and then billing them for it. It's kind of like going to a party, participating in a few minutes of small talk, and walking out with 3,000 dollars.

PSYCHIC
-If you were truly qualified for this vocation, you wouldn't be reading this book—you'd already **know** what was in it.

PSYCHOLOGIST
-Here, you will do what a Psychiatrist does. However, **you're** smart enough to realize you don't need to expend time and money for Med school in order to ask someone questions, pretend to be interested, and walk out with 3,000 dollars.

PUBLIC RELATIONS SPECIALIST
-A skilled professional who elevates the "Art of B.S." to a science. For example, it would be your job to make the public realize that a major plane crash or oil spill is actually **good** for them, and that they should be grateful to your company for providing new jobs like **Oil Slick Cleaner-uppers.**

PUBLIC WORKS EMPLOYEE
-To work in this area, you must pass the "Sitting Under A Big Shade Tree In Your Truck" exam. Test sections include Breakfast, Snack Time, Brunch, Coffee Break, Lunch, Tea Time, Advanced Snack, Dinner, After-Dinner Thermos, Dessert, and Midnight Snack. Bonus: Dunkin Donuts.

PUBLISHER
-A wonderfully nice person who assists a Writer in countless ways, in exchange for the Writer kissing up to them.

PYROTECHNICIAN
-You will work in the intricate and dangerous field of fireworks presentations. If you're a klutz, you should skip this occupation and stick to sparklers.

"It was to later be known as the July 3rd Incident"

QUALITY CONTROL EXPERT

-These people spend years in collegiate industrial engineering programs. Upon graduation, they proceed directly to fast-food restaurants, where they're put in charge of the "Making sure your burger takes an excessively long time to get to you" system.

RABBI

-If you can take a brief message, and stretch it into a 45-minute monologue, you could be Rabbi material. If you can say the word **Sukkot** without breaking into laughter, you're **definitely** Rabbi material.

RACE CAR DRIVER
-If you enjoy risking your life by screeching around in a speeding car, why not just flag down a New York City taxi?

RACK JOBBER
-This occupation wins the award for sounding most like an illegal or perverted activity. In fact, though, a Rack Jobber just stocks store displays with a company's product, such as Hanes panty hose. Of course, with this in mind, you might **prefer** having people think you're a criminal or a pervert.

REAL ESTATE BROKER
-This is a person who describes a cinder block on an empty lot as a **Fixer-upper** and a house next to a leaky fire hydrant as **Waterfront.**

RECREATION WORKER
-A classic oxymoron. You work so people can play. *(See Saw)*

RED CROSS WORKER
-If Irwin Allen disaster movies and Special Reports get your blood flowing, you'll find your thrill here.

REFEREE, PRO FOOTBALL
-A much tougher job in recent years, now that instant replays point out just how bad your calls really are.

REGIONAL PLANNER
-In this field, you'll study a geographical area, and plan exactly where houses and businesses should be built so that driving **anywhere** takes you through at least three school zones.

REPAIRMAN, MAJOR APPLIANCE
-Not for the shy person. Union rules dictate that "your pants must sit at least 1 1/2 inches below the top of the crack of your rear end at all times." (Is it any wonder why the Maytag repairman is so lonely?)

REPAIRMAN, MISCELLANEOUS
-Here, you will go out and fix an object that the man of the house tried desperately to repair, but subsequently destroyed. By saving his total embarrassment, you may double your usual fee.

RESEARCHER
-A person who knows way more about a subject than anyone else really cares to know.

RESERVATION/TICKET AGENT
-It's your duty to explain to potential airline passengers that the fare quoted in the ad is available, as long as the passenger makes reservations 230 days in advance; flies between Tuesday and Wednesday but not on a weekday; has no children or carry-on luggage, nor any stored luggage; must sit in a special smoking section if a non-smoker; must provide own food and drink, and enough for all other passengers; and if they want to change times or dates, risk death by eating extra servings of airplane food.

RESTROOM ATTENDANT
-Unless you're going to help shake it or blot it dry, you really don't serve much of a purpose other than making those who use the restroom paranoid.

ROOFER
-In this business, you keep a roof over your head by keeping a roof under your feet.

$ALESPERSON, STORE (<u>NOT</u> ON COMMISSION)

-You're not expected to ring up any purchases until the customer actually **rips** the romance novel from your hands.

SALESPERSON, STORE (<u>ON</u> COMMISSION)

-You must master phrases like "That red polka dot dress, combined with that brown mullet-skinned overcoat, *is* you." *(See Actor)*

SANTA CLAUS

-A good job for the guy whose beer belly has expanded with each week of football season.

SCHOOL BAND DIRECTOR

-An excellent position for the hearing-impaired. *(Note: After five years of high-pitched clarinet squeaks, you <u>will</u> be hearing-impaired.)*

SCHOOL CAFETERIA SERVER

-A closed profession. This is the only successful human cloning experiment on record, right down to the hair nets.

SCHOOL CAREER COUNSELOR
-If you're not quite sure what career to settle on, this is the job for you. You won't become any less confused, but at least you can screw up thousands of others, so you're all on about the same level.

SCHOOL CUSTODIAN
-There are actually only six School Custodians in the nation. Visit any school and you'll see—they're the same guys who were at **your** school.

SCHOOL GUIDANCE COUNSELOR
-It will be your job to stress to students the importance of taking a class like Calculus rather than an elective. After all, those of us in the real world know how many times each and every day we need to use those logarithms and derivatives.

SCHOOL PRINCIPAL
-To assist kids with proper spelling, this occupation often stresses the "pal" part on the end of **Principal.** Yeah, that's just what pals are for—to paddle your butt when you do something wrong.

SCREENWRITER
-A wonderful profession. You just write down your ideas, and wait for your paycheck. (Give or take 14.3 million rejection letters that you find through your bi-hourly visits to the mailbox.)

SECRETARY
-In this position, you will be required to take notes, type letters, and RUN THE COMPANY. In return, your boss will buy you a plant on Secretary's Day. **If** you're lucky.

SECURITY GUARD
-This is the 97-pound, uniformed (and uninformed) guy who walks through the mall with his tin badge and Radio Shack walkie-talkie, protecting (**guffaw, chuckle**) shoppers. In times of danger or confrontation, he can often be found hiding under the sales table at Sears.

SEISMOLOGIST
-You'll have a very active sex life—people will sleep with you just to see what they attained on the Richter scale.

SELF-EMPLOYED WORKER
-**Advantage:** It's hard to be late for work.
Disadvantage: The office Christmas party may be on the dull side.

SEX SURROGATE
-A Prostitute with a Masters (and Johnson) degree.

SHOE SALESPERSON
-Psychologically demeaning, in that you must kneel at the feet of countless men, women, and children. Of course, it *is* good practice for married life.

SHRINER
-These volunteers help the medical community by acting as human guinea pigs. As part of an ongoing study, the men are given massive amounts of alcohol, then squeezed into miniature cars, and let loose in the middle of parades.

SHUTTLE BUS DRIVER
-We've always been taught to never pick up strangers. But that's exactly what you'd be doing all day long in this job. Do yourself a favor and tell your mom you're a Mall Security Guard and that if there's any trouble, you'll be safe under the Sears sales table.

SIGN MAKER
-If customers have trouble finding your shop, you're not very good.

SINGER
-This is a person who can make his or her voice glide continuously up dozens of octaves on **Star Search**, until the audience applauds and dogs throughout the city begin chasing bus benches.

SKYWRITER
-If you're a poor speller, this occupation can be **real** embarrassing.

SOCIAL WORKER
-Social Work is kind of an interesting job, in that with the **wonderful** salary you receive, you can look forward to someday needing social assistance yourself.

SOCIOLOGIST
-You will spend your entire life trying to figure out why people in elevators always stand quietly facing the doors. This is all you will study. Ever.

SOLE PROPRIETOR
1) A self-employed person with a fax machine.
2) A guy who owns and operates his own fish market.

SPEAKER OF THE HOUSE
-For years, this has been one of the President's wacky Washington wild men. However, this position is no longer actually accessible. Since 1975, you've been witnessing the finest in audio-animatronics.

HELP! I AM OUT OF GAS

SPECIAL EFFECTS TECHNICIAN
-With enough dedication, maybe you can become that Special Effects Technician who discovers how to make Roseanne Arnold appear **thin** on camera.

SPECIAL EFFECTS MODEL BUILDER
-Here, you'll use 6-inch models to simulate something much, much larger. This training might also be handy in your personal life.

SPEECH THERAPIST
-You'll work with patients like heavyweight boxer Mike Tyson to make him sound even wimpier, which in turn helps him deceive his opponents and win fights.

SPOKESMODEL (STAR SEARCH)
-Not the brightest of persons. The 3-way bulb in their brain only works on **Low.**

SPORTSCASTER
-There's a lot of competition in this field, but you've gotta suck in your gut, stick it out, and hang in there, playing all four quarters right up the middle. Once you're cranked up and you've got that momentum back so you're on the top of the game, you can go all the way for the big score—a **real** job.

STATISTICIAN
-Statisticians are fun at parties. They can tell you that your chances of getting lucky that night are nil...plus or minus 5 percent.

STENOGRAPHER
-Your job is to translate entire speeches into things like ^~\ | | {<..!!~~ in a matter of seconds. However, anyone who can move his or her fingers that fast could be making a lot more money at another profession.

STOCKBROKER
-"Now is the best time to invest." If you can say that phrase 5 days a week, 52 weeks a year, for the rest of your life, you've got yourself a job.

STORE OWNER
-If you can endure the phrase *"Just looking"* thousands of times each day without slapping the customer, you've found your niche.

STRIPPER
-Look at it this way—How many other jobs can you get strangers to slip $10 bills in your undergarments? (OK, maybe *I.R.S. Agent*)

STUNT PERSON
-If you're having a tough time deciding whether you want to be a movie star, or whether you want to commit suicide, here's the perfect compromise.

SUBSTITUTE TEACHER
-Here's one job where the job itself encourages others to torment you and make your life a living hell. "Y'know—Miss Brennan always lets us go out to Baskin Robbins the second half of the period."

SUMO WRESTLER
-You're appropriate in this capacity if:
1) Nobody has ever said to you, "Nice butt!";
2) As a kid, you beat up Toyotas; and
3) When you were born, you were heavier than your Mom.

SUPERVISOR
-This is a person who clawed their way to the top, and will **never** let you forget it.

SURFER
-Yo, Dude, Like if it's that gnarly time when ya gotta find a job that's bitchin, catch a plane (or a wave) to Hawaii and like, become a professional Surfer Dude, like, fer sure.

"So, what line of work are you in?"

SURGEON
-A helpful hint: If you're in the habit of saying "Whoops!" after making a mistake, you'll want to stay away from surgery involving local anesthesia.

SURGEON GENERAL, U.S.
-Your sole purpose is to tell people that what they like will kill them.

TAILOR

-If you enjoy touching complete strangers in sensitive areas, this is the field you should enter. But remember, you must have **very** steady hands. A shaky Tailor armed with pins and clips can make Barry White sing like Alvin and the Chipmunks.

TALK-SHOW HOST, DAYTIME
-Good employment opportunities are available here, at least until that fateful day when we run out of bisexual midget Catholic mud-wrestlers who suffocated their ex-mistresses' mutant gerbils with leather.

TALK-SHOW HOST, DONAHUE SUCCESSOR
-With enough years of training, you too can learn to interrupt every interesting moment for a commercial break.

TALK-SHOW HOST, LATE NIGHT
-You must have the expertise to look truly interested when interviewing Terri Garr for the 43rd time in one month.

TAXI DRIVER
-It's your job to find the longest route between two points, without having your passengers catch on.

TEACHER, ELEMENTARY SCHOOL
-In this teaching job, the youth and innocence of your students allows you to avoid the heavy stuff. At this level, you can simply lecture on crime, sexual diseases, and drug use.

TEACHER, JUNIOR HIGH SCHOOL
-Being a Junior High Teacher lets you combine the art of education with the skill of self-defense techniques, for an occupation never devoid of excitement.

TEACHER, SENIOR HIGH SCHOOL
-It's your job to put just enough academic pressure on your students in these very formative years, so that for the rest of their lives, they'll have one recurring nightmare: Having to take a final exam in a class they forgot to attend all semester.

TELEMARKETER (PHONE SALESPERSON)
-If you're considering this job, you should be aware that the term **Telemarketer** was created in recent years as most people, having their eating, sleeping,

and sexual activities interrupted, began feeling free to "tell-a-marketer" what he could do with his once-in-a-lifetime offer.

TELEPHONE LINE REPAIRMAN
-Don't waste your money dialing those silly "900" numbers. This occupation lets you climb a tall pole in the neighborhood and peer into anybody's window, while using your magic little handset to tap into **their** "900" calls.

TELEVANGELIST
-Brothers and sisters! Do you heeeear the calling?! Is this vocation screeeeaming for your soul?! Do you have a special love for kinky perversions and other people's money?! Then Yeh-ess! I say Yeh-ess! Join us today! Take up a precious channel on the cable box, and embezzle **millions,** I say **millions** of dollars from gullible idiots naaa-tionwide.

TEST PILOT
-If a tall, slow-moving Ferris wheel is enough to make you nauseous, you'll probably want to steer clear of this occupation.

THESAURUS WRITER
-An Author, Editor, Creator, Hack, Penman, Copyist, Publisher, or Transcriber.

TIME-LIFE OPERATOR
-Not quite up to speed with the rest of the world. Their VCR's blink 11:00, 11:00, 11:00....

TOLL COLLECTOR, HIGHWAY
-*Thank you... Thank you... Thank you....*
That's the job.

TOUR GUIDE
-A role that never has to get boring. Visitors put their trust in your knowledge. Screw 'em. "On the left, you'll see the pink art deco house Abe Lincoln and Richard Nixon were born in...."

TRAFFIC COP
-The perfect occupation for those who'd like to be an Orchestra Conductor, but can't keep a beat.

TRAFFIC SIGNAL PROGRAMMER
-In this career, you will work with inanimate objects to piss off humans.

TRANSLATOR
-This is a person who translates a foreign language that you don't understand into English that you don't understand.

TRAPEZE ARTIST
-While the work is far from plentiful, there *is* a need for artists who paint trapezes.

TRASH COLLECTOR
-The only occupation left that requires real men .... Men who can mangle your metal trash cans

beyond recognition... Men who can take your dilapidated old patio furniture and twist it back into shape for themselves... Men who can get a whiff of 6-day-old meat loaf and not puke.

TRAVEL AGENT

-It's your job to make sure that the vacation your client has saved for all year is a complete nightmare. At least five times during the trip, they should be asked, "Could it be under a different name?"

TREE SURGEON

-So Mom and Dad wanted you to become a Doctor, but you weren't too excited about that whole medical thing? **This** is your career. Your parents can say their kid's a surgeon, while you can rest assured your weekend football games will never be interrupted by some stupid beeper.

TRUCK DRIVER

-Before certification, you must be proficient at:
A) Speaking incoherently into a C.B. radio;
B) Following traffic at a one-car distance
   for every 80 m.p.h.; and
C) Looking like if the truck won't start, you could
   push it.

TV NETWORK PRESIDENT

-This individual has the most up-to-date information on what Americans want to watch, and then chooses the opposite.

**MPIRE**

-Depending on what call you make at any given time, one group of fans will detest you, and the other group really won't care a whole lot about you either. You can't win.

UNDERTAKER
-A good profession, in that customer complaints are **very** rare.

UNDERWRITER
-It's your job to write up insurance policies so that in the event of an unfortunate incident, the policyholder is sure to fall into either an exemption, addendum, or S.O.L.um.

UNEMPLOYED PERSON
-Ahh, the most effective way to avoid an annoying boss and a half-hour lunch. Besides, how else can you catch up on reruns of **Gilligan's Island** and **I Love Lucy?**

U.S. NUCLEAR COMMAND POST OPERATOR
-This is one profession which deserves much respect.... Not because of the immense responsibilities on your shoulders— just because any sane person would be foolish to get you **really** pissed off.

UNIVERSITY PRESIDENT
-A Beggar with a mascot.

USED CAR SALESMAN
-One of the most ridiculed jobs in history. And for good reason. If the phrase **"previously-owned"** sounds legit to you, or if you feel people too often think of the word **shyster** in a negative light, you're just the breed this field needs.

USHER, MOVIE THEATER
1) These are usually the guys who aren't quite on the ball enough to figure out that the Jerry Lewis who hosts the MDA Telethon is the same Jerry Lewis who starred in all the movies with Dean Martin.
2) A sadist with a flashlight.

# VALET PARKING ATTENDANT

-Advanced parking attendants can get a car up to 65 m.p.h. in a forty-foot lot. But even if you're a beginner, your in-car training is protected by the small print on the back of the ticket stub given to the car owner: "Valet park at your own risk. Valet driver may use your vehicle for personal needs, including but not limited to errands, jackrabbit starts, figure-eights, giving a lift to a friend, slalom courses, canyon jumping, and testing crash dummies. Additionally, all valuables left in car automatically become the property of Valet Driver."

VENDING MACHINE SERVICEMAN
-A lucrative position if you're an experienced Serviceman, in that by rigging the machine to dispense items every **other** time money is put in, you get to keep the extra change.

VETERINARIAN
-One step below **Doctor** and one step above **Botanist.** A good profession for anyone who became aroused while watching **Doctor Dolittle.**

VICE PRESIDENT OF THE U.S.
-*(As we went to press, we were still trying to find out the duties of this job.)*

VOCATIONAL SCHOOL INSTRUCTOR
-Through nighttime classes, you'll help individuals get out of their dead-end jobs, and into new dead-end jobs. You'll teach courses such as "Modeling with Advanced Car Repair/Paramedic Skills" at a place called something like "The Bumbling Institute." Your enrollment motto will be, "If you're breathing—We're accepting!"

VOLUNTEER
-These generous people give their time to worthy causes, asking for absolutely nothing in return, which is nice. Absurd, but nice.

WAITER/WAITRESS

-In this position, you're like a good parent, taking care of somebody's every need. The only difference is that here, you're not allowed to slap them.

WAITRESS AT 24-HOUR RESTAURANT THAT RHYMES WITH "LENNY'S"

-It's a little easier to break in here. The only requirement is that you must have open sores on at least 3/4 of your body.

WAREHOUSE SECURITY GUARD

-An excellent job for the recently-deceased.

WEATHERMAN

-If you know nothing about meteorology, but **do** know you aspire to become a Comedian or Talk-Show Host, this is the position for you.

WEDDING PHOTOGRAPHER

-This is usually a shady character who takes some pictures of your wedding for around $30,000, and then keeps the negatives for his own undisclosed use.

WEDDING PLANNER
-Do you live for celebrations and merriment? Have you always been a big-time partier? Work in this business a few months, and you'll be so sick of **other** people having fun, the letters **R.S.V.P.** will make you physically ill.

WINDOW DRESSER
-Perfect for those with deviant sexual tendencies. In this specialty, you'll dress and undress mannequins while a crowd forms to watch.

WINDOW WASHER
-Here's a specialty where your parents' lecturing, "Don't stare" pays off. While dangling against windows, you must make it look like glare is preventing you from seeing in, while in fact, there's a new show every window.

WINDOW WASHER DRESSER
-For the extremely wealthy Window Washer, you will select his outfits and make sure everything comes together.

WORD PROCESSOR
-The modern name for a *Typist.* You see, by providing you with a nice title and some fancy business cards, your employer can get away with giving you a lower salary, severe back pain, and permanent eye damage.

WRESTLER, PROFESSIONAL
-Mother Nature's reminder of what we would've been without evolution.

WRITER
-As a Writer, you sit down and try to decide what kind of book people could really use. Then your Mastercard bill arrives, and you opt to write something that will sell, Sell, SELL!

-RAY TECHNOLOGIST

-This is an individual who **once was** a Ray Technologist.

XXX-RAY TECHNOLOGIST

-This is generally an X-Ray Technologist who asks you to disrobe thirty minutes before the actual procedure. And the only thing needing an X-ray is your thumb.

YARDMAN
-A Gardener in Palm Beach.

YO-YO EXPERT
-In this role, you're announcing to the world that you have entirely too much time on your hands. Instead, go walk the dog, rock the baby, or travel around the world.

ZOO KEEPER

-Before you can be a Zoo Keeper, you must be a Zoo Getter. Then just keep it.

ZOOLOGIST

-People in this profession are notorious for having low self-esteem, in that they're always listed *last* in career guides.

CONCLUSION

Now that your mind is overflowing with ideas for your new career, it's time to get off your duff and forge ahead. Go out there and show the world what you can do!

Of course, you'll probably want to hang onto this book just in case your newly-chosen occupation turns out to be the biggest mistake of your life.

But no matter what happens, the most important element in choosing your new line of work is maintaining a positive attitude. With this healthy frame of mind, the career-hunting process should be fun and exciting.

Lastly, always remember: YOU CAN BE ANYTHING YOU WANT TO BE, except perhaps a Sumo Wrestler.

Good luck with your new career!

ABOUT THE AUTHOR

Bob Glickman began trying to write humor in elementary school. He succeeded about ten years later, at the University of Florida, where he became the Head Writer for the **Gator Growl** homecoming show, and had a humor column in the school newspaper. After graduating with two B.S. degrees, which seemed quite apropos, he began writing for comedians such as Joan Rivers and Jay Leno for their monologues on NBC's **Tonight Show.** He has twice won the Comedy Division of the Florida Screenwriter's Competition, and has written for the nationally-syndicated comedy/game show **Sweethearts.** His previous books include **The Worst Baby Name Book** and **The Comedy Material Sourcebook.** Bob is single, but has a lovely imaginary girlfriend named Bambi.

TITLES BY CCC PUBLICATIONS

–NEW BOOKS–

WORK IS AN OCCUPATIONAL HAZARD

HOW TO <u>REALLY</u> PARTY!!!

THE PEOPLE WATCHER'S FIELD GUIDE

NEVER A DULL CARD

THE ABSOLUTE **LAST CHANCE** DIET BOOK

HUSBANDS FROM HELL

HORMONES FROM HELL
(The Ultimate <u>Women's</u> Humor Book!)

FOR **MEN** ONLY
(How To Survive Marriage)

THE Unofficial WOMEN'S DIVORCE GUIDE

HOW TO TALK YOUR WAY OUT OF A TRAFFIC TICKET

WHAT DO WE DO NOW??
(The Complete Guide For All New Parents Or Parents-To-Be)

THE SUPERIOR PERSON'S GUIDE TO EVERYDAY IRRITATIONS

YOUR GUIDE TO CORPORATE SURVIVAL

GIFTING RIGHT
(How To Give A Great Gift Every Time! For Any Occasion! And On Any Budget!)

--COMING SOON--

THE GUILT BAG [Accessory Item]

IT'S BETTER TO BE OVER THE HILL--THAN UNDER IT

THE BOTTOM HALF

THE UGLY TRUTH ABOUT MEN

--BEST SELLERS--

NO HANG-UPS (Funny Answering Machine Messages)
NO HANG-UPS II
NO HANG-UPS III
GETTING EVEN WITH THE ANSWERING MACHINE
HOW TO GET EVEN WITH YOUR EXes
HOW TO SUCCEED IN SINGLES BARS
TOTALLY OUTRAGEOUS BUMPER-SNICKERS
THE "MAGIC BOOKMARK" BOOK COVER
[Accessory Item]

--CASSETTES--

NO HANG-UPS TAPES (Funny, Pre-recorded Answering Machine Messages   With Hilarious <u>Sound Effects</u>) -- In Male or Female Voices

- Vol. I: GENERAL MESSAGES
- Vol. II: BUSINESS MESSAGES
- Vol. III: 'R' RATED MESSAGES
- Vol. IV: SOUND EFFECTS ONLY
- Vol. V: CELEBRI-TEASE
  (Celebrity Impersonations)

CAREER NOTES:

CAREER NOTES:

CAREER NOTES:

CAREER NOTES:

CAREER NOTES: